THIS CANDLEWICK BOOK BELONGS TO:

_____

_____

_____

First U.S. paperback edition 2008

Library of Congress Cataloging-in-Publication Data is available.
Library of Congress Catalog Card Number 2007025611
ISBN 978-0-7636-3559-6 (hardcover)
ISBN 978-0-7636-4031-6 (paperback)

WKT 24 23 22 21 20
16 15 14 13 12

Printed in Shenzhen, Guangdong, China

This book was typeset in ITCKabel.
The illustrations were created digitally.

Candlewick Press
99 Dover Street
Somerville, Massachusetts 02144

visit us at www.candlewick.com

CANDLEWICK PRESS

For Annie

The author and publisher would like
to thank Sue Ellis at the Centre for Literacy in
Primary Education, Martin Jenkins, and Paul Harrison
for their invaluable input and guidance
during the making of this book.

OSCAR and the MOTH

A BOOK ABOUT LIGHT AND DARK

Geoff Waring

One summer evening, Oscar lay on the warm back step.

Moth was just waking up.
"Where does the sun go at night?" Oscar asked her.
"It doesn't go anywhere," Moth answered, "but the Earth is always turning around. Now it's turning slowly away from the sun."

Oscar was surprised.
"I'm not turning around!" he said.

"We can't feel it," Moth said, "but we can see it. When our side of the Earth turns toward the sun, it gets light. And when it turns away again, it gets dark."

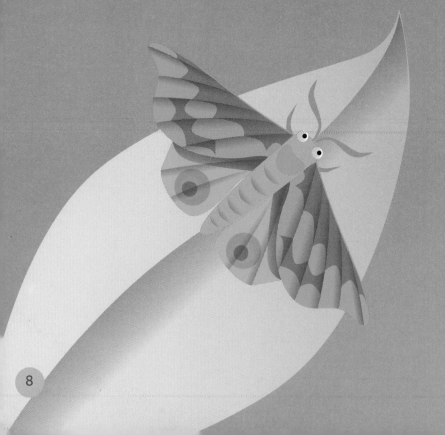

MORNING

LUNCHTIME

EVENING

Oscar sat up. "I'm cold," he said, shivering.

"It's because we've turned away from the sun," said Moth, "and now we don't have the sun's light or its warmth. That's why it's almost always colder at night than during the day."

Just then, the outside
lamp came on.
Moth flew toward it.

"I sleep during the day,"
she said, "so I don't see
the sun. But I love
the lamp's light
and its warmth."

Oscar looked up.
He could feel the lamp's
warm light on his face.
"Is the lamp as hot as
the sun?" he asked.

"No," said Moth.
"The sun is our
brightest and
hottest light."

"Are all lights hot?" Oscar asked.

"Not all," said Moth, "but many are."

Oscar climbed off the step and looked out at the starry sky.
Moth flew down to join him. "You can only see the stars
at night," she said.

"They are always shining, but you can't see them during the day because of the light from the sun."

Our sun is a star, too. It is closer to the Earth than other stars are, so its light is much brighter to us than theirs and it looks very big.

17

Moth flew toward the street.
"Without the sun's light,
we need other lights
to help us," she said.

18

Oscar could see
the lights of an airplane,
a streetlight, and
a lamp in the window.

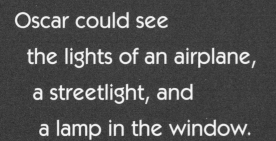

"What are those little lights?"
he asked. "They're dancing!"
"Those are fireflies," Moth said. "They are
beetles that can make their own light."

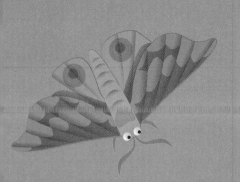

And she told Oscar about how some living creatures make light in their own bodies.

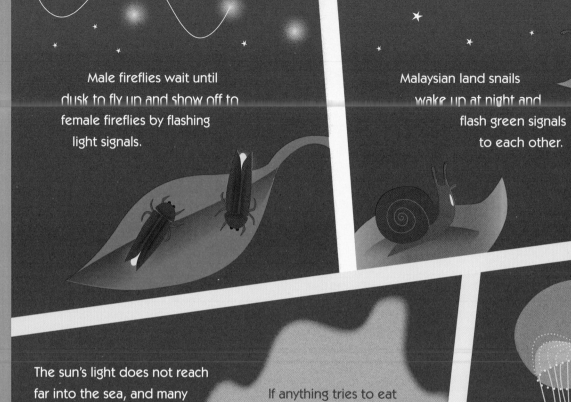

Male fireflies wait until dusk to fly up and show off to female fireflies by flashing light signals.

Malaysian land snails wake up at night and flash green signals to each other.

The sun's light does not reach far into the sea, and many sea creatures make their own light.

If anything tries to eat a swordfish squid, it squirts a glowing ink cloud. This dazzles the hungry fish, allowing the squid to escape.

The rim of a crystal jellyfish glows green when it is disturbed.

There's a poisonous millipede found in California that lights up at night to warn other animals not to eat it.

The anglerfish lives in the deep sea. It has a big spine on its head with a tip that glows blue-green. The tip acts as "bait" to lure other fish, which the anglerfish then eats.

"I wish I could glow too," Oscar said.

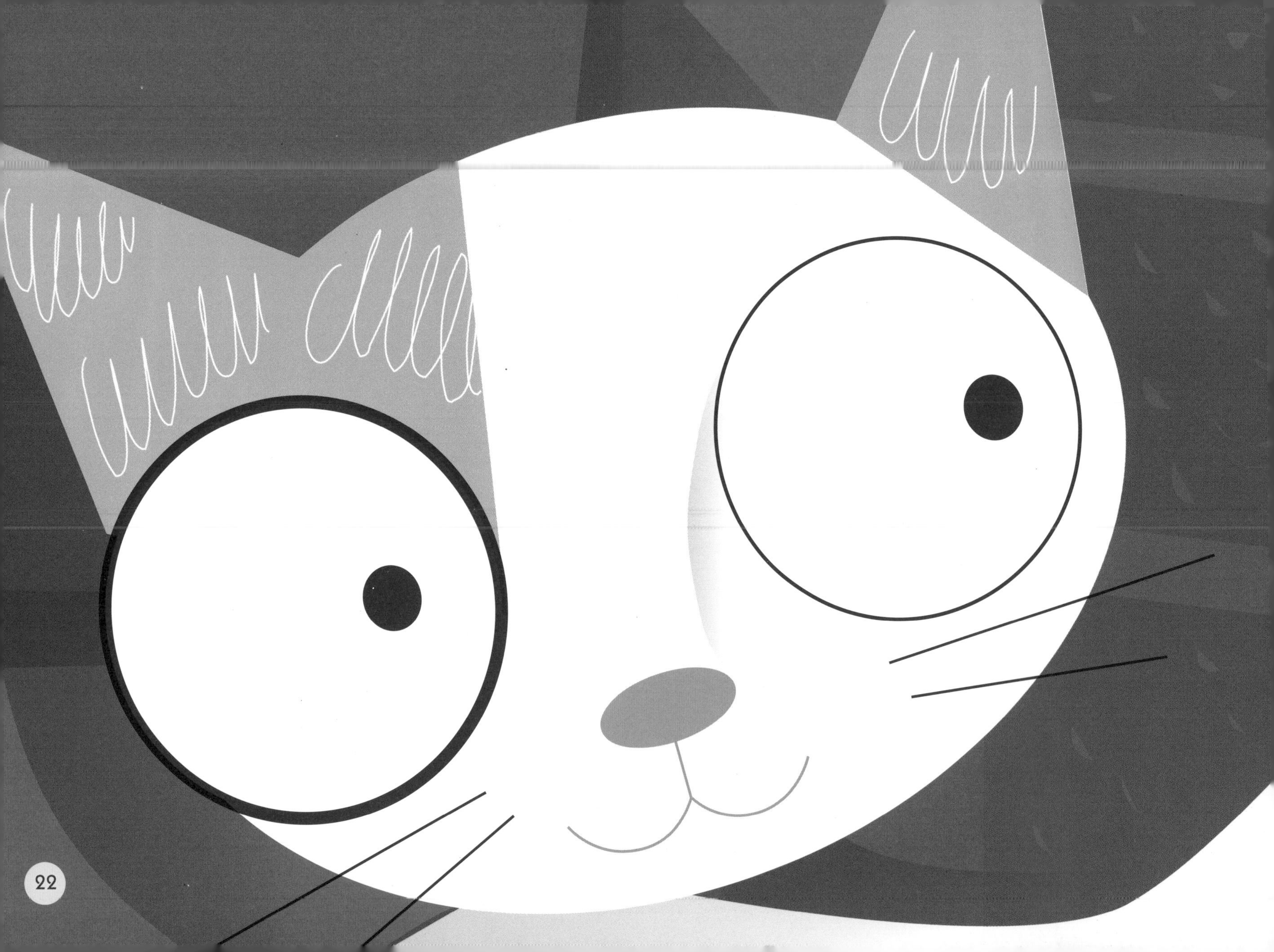

Just then, Oscar noticed something swooping around. "Look, Moth. There's your shadow!" he called.

"My body is stopping some of the light
from reaching the wall," Moth said.
"It leaves a dark patch
that's the same shape as me."

"Where's *my* shadow?" asked Oscar.
"If you stand up," Moth said, "you'll see."

Oscar got up.

There was an
Oscar-shaped shadow
on the wall!

Oscar lay down again (and so did his shadow).

He closed his eyes.

The dark behind his eyelids made him feel sleepy.

"Is it nearly morning?" he said with a yawn.

"Not yet, Oscar," said Moth.

But Oscar didn't hear her. He was already dreaming about the bright sun, the shining stars, and deep-sea fishes.

Thinking about light . . .

Talking with Moth, Oscar found out that . . .

Light comes from many different sources.

The sun

Lamps

Stars

Living creatures

Some lights are brighter than others.

Many lights are hot.
The sun's heat means that it is usually warmer during the day than at night.

Warm

Cold

What lights can you see around you now?
(If the sun is shining, don't look at it directly—it's too bright.)

Index

Look up the pages to find out about these "light and dark" things:

brightness 14, 17, 27, 28
cold 11, 28
day 11, 12, 17, 28
Earth 7–8, 17
glowing 20–21

lamps 12, 14, 19, 28–29
night 7, 11, 16, 20–21, 28–29
shadows 23, 25–26, 29
shining 17, 27, 28

stars 16–17, 27, 28–29
sun 7–8, 11–12, 14, 17–18, 27–29
warmth 7, 11–12, 14–15, 28

and dark

Many lights are easier to see at night.

Stars

Fireflies

When we don't have the sun's light, we need other lights.

Airplane lights

Streetlight

When something blocks the light, it makes a shadow.

The dark can make us feel sleepy.

Do you turn off the lights in your bedroom before you go to sleep at night? If you keep a night-light on, does it make shadows?

Oscar thinks light and dark are great! Do you think so, too?

Geoff Waring studied graphics in college and has worked as an art director at *Elle*, *Red*, and *Vogue Australia* and as design director of *British Vogue*. He is currently creative director of *Glamour* magazine. He is the author and illustrator of the Oscar books, as well as the illustrator of *Black Meets White* by Justine Fontes. He says that the Oscar books are based on his own cat, Oskar. Geoff Waring lives in London.